my itty-bitty bio

Mahatma Gandhi

Cherry Lake Press

Published in the United States of America by Cherry Lake Publishing Group
Ann Arbor, Michigan
www.cherrylakepublishing.com

Reading Adviser: Marla Conn, MS Ed., Literacy specialist, Read-Ability, Inc.
Book Designer: Jennifer Wahl
Illustrator: Jeff Bane

Photo Credits: ©tantrik71/shutterstock, 5, 21; ©Radiokafka/shutterstock, 7; ©Public Domain/Wikimedia, 9; ©Public Domain/Wikimedia, 11; ©Public Domain/Public.Resource.Org/flickr, 13; ©Public Domain/Wikimedia, 15, 22; ©Public Domain/Wikimedia, 17; ©Public Domain/Wikimedia, 19, 23; Jeff Bane, Cover, 1, 10, 12, 16

Cherry Lake Press is an imprint of Cherry Lake Publishing Group.

Library of Congress Cataloging-in-Publication Data

Names: Pincus, Meeg, author. | Bane, Jeff, 1957- illustrator.
Title: Mahatma Gandhi / by Meeg Pincus, ; illustrated by Jeff Bane.
Description: Ann Arbor, Michigan : Cherry Lake Publishing, 2021. | Series: My itty-bitty bio | Includes index. | Audience: Grades K-1 | Summary: "The My Itty-Bitty Bio series are biographies for the earliest readers. This book examines the life of social activist Mahatma Gandhi in a simple, age-appropriate way that will help young readers develop word recognition and reading skills. Includes a table of contents, author biography, timeline, glossary, index, and other informative backmatter"-- Provided by publisher.
Identifiers: LCCN 2020035876 (print) | LCCN 2020035877 (ebook) | ISBN 9781534179929 (hardcover) | ISBN 9781534181632 (paperback) | ISBN 9781534180932 (pdf) | ISBN 9781534182646 (ebook)
Subjects: LCSH: Gandhi, Mahatma, 1869-1948--Juvenile literature. | Pacifists--India--Biography--Juvenile literature. | Nonviolence--India--History--20th century--Juvenile literature.
Classification: LCC DS481.G3 P55 2021 (print) | LCC DS481.G3 (ebook) | DDC 954.03/5092 [B]--dc23
LC record available at https://lccn.loc.gov/2020035876
LC ebook record available at https://lccn.loc.gov/2020035877

Printed in the United States of America
Corporate Graphics

table of contents

About the author: Meeg Pincus has been a writer, editor, and educator for 25 years. She loves to write inspiring stories for kids about people, animals, and our planet. She lives near San Diego, California, where she enjoys the beach, reading, singing, and her family.

About the illustrator: Jeff Bane and his two business partners own a studio along the American River in Folsom, California, home of the 1849 Gold Rush. When Jeff's not sketching or illustrating for clients, he's either swimming or kayaking in the river to relax.

my story

I was born in India. It was 1869.
I had three **siblings**.

My family was Hindu. We prayed, **fasted**, and did not eat meat.

I was very shy. But that didn’t stop me. I became a **lawyer**. I saw people of color being badly treated in South Africa. I wanted to help them. I led my first peaceful **protest**.

What would you protest?

England owned India and made **strict** laws. I wanted my country to be free. I led more protests.

I wrote books. I wrote about peace and change.

How can you make
change happen peacefully?

I led the Salt March.
We protested England's **tax**
on salt in India.

English police put me in jail. I fasted in protest. People around the world supported me.

India finally won its freedom.
We won with no **violence**.
It took 30 years.

I died in 1948. Martin Luther King Jr. was a **civil rights** leader. He used my **methods** for peaceful change. Leaders still use them today.

What would you like to ask me?

timeline

1930

1860

Born
1869

1947

1960

Died
1948

glossary & index

glossary

civil rights (SIV-uhl RITES) the right of all people to be treated equally under the law

fasted (FAST-id) stopped eating for a time

lawyer (LOI-ur) a person who has studied the law and can help people

methods (METH-uhdz) ways of doing something

protest (PROH-test) a march, demonstration, or statement against something

siblings (SIB-lingz) brothers and sisters

strict (STRIKT) must be followed

tax (TAX) money collected by the government from people and businesses

violence (VYE-uh-luhns) the use of physical force to cause harm

index